INSTANT HAPPY

Notes

AND OTHER SURPRISES
TO MAKE YOU SMILE

 sourcebooks

Copyright © 2017 by Sourcebooks, Inc.
Cover and internal design © 2017 by Sourcebooks, Inc.
Internal artwork by individual artists: John Aardema, Bridget M. Alexander, Elizabeth Boyer, Susan Busch, Catherine Casalino Design, Jennifer K. Beal Davis, Matt Davis, Maggie Edkins, Cassie Gutman, Travis Hasenour, Nicole Hower, Krista Joy Johnson, Kelly Lawler, Michelle McAvoy, Danielle McNaughton, Lin Miceli, Benjamin Nelson, Kay Birkner, Heather Morris, Bethany Orlowski, Ben Ouart, Jenna Quatraro, Jillian Rahn, Kerri Resnick, Kandi Rich, Tina Silva, Becca Sage, Eliza Smith, Allison Sundstrom, Amanda Skolek, Brittany Vibbert, Christine Webster
Internal images © Freepik.com, Unsplash.com, Merfin/GettyImages, sundrawalex/GettyImages, Vit_Mar/GettyImages, Vanzyst/GettyImages, Ukususha/Thinkstock, Julia_Henze/Thinkstock, Vioricalonescu/Thinkstock, speakingtomato/Thinkstock, artJazz/Thinkstock, topform84/Thinkstock, beatpavel/Thinkstock, Martyshova/Thinkstock, yayayoyo/Thinkstock, Lostanastacia/Thinkstock, nata789/Thinkstock, chereshneva/Thinkstock

Sourcebooks and the colophon are registered trademarks of Sourcebooks, Inc.

All rights reserved. No part of this book may be reproduced in any form or by any electronic or mechanical means including information storage and retrieval systems—except in the case of brief quotations embodied in critical articles or reviews—without permission in writing from its publisher, Sourcebooks, Inc.

Published by Sourcebooks, Inc.
P.O. Box 4410, Naperville, Illinois 60567-4410
(630) 961-3900
Fax: (630) 961-2168
www.sourcebooks.com

Printed and bound in China.
LEO 10 9 8 7 6 5 4 3 2 1

This collection of notes has been lovingly created by the dreamers, designers, and artists at Sourcebooks for you, our readers. Plus, we were able to include work from a number of friends who share our belief that books change lives. Each unique design is a vision from one of the many people who have the privilege of making books every day. We hope the notes within spark true happiness and create the unique magic only found between the pages of a book.

Thank you

for being a part of our story—now go get happy!

Brittany Vibbert

Brittany Vibbert, Art Director

Meaghan Gibbons

Meaghan Gibbons, Editor

BRIGHTEN UP YOUR DAY

boost the happiness around you with these feel-good notes! You'll find unexpected compliments, much-needed encouragement, lighthearted fun, and silly doodles that are sure to make you grin. The sole purpose of this chunky, compact book is to boost your mood—just think of it as your best friend who will bring you instant happy wherever you go!

THE BEST WAY TO PREDICT THE FUTURE IS TO CREATE it
—ABRAHAM LINCOLN

MAKE TODAY COUNT

Every Day IS A Fresh START

Light tomorrow with today.

Elizabeth Barrett Browning

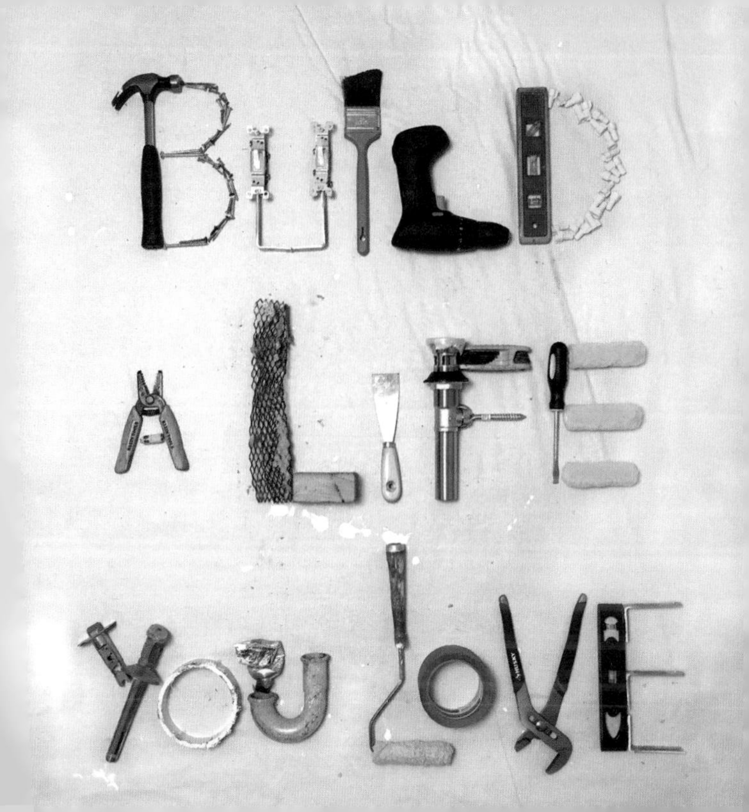
BUILD
A LIFE
YOU LOVE

CARPE THAT DIEM!

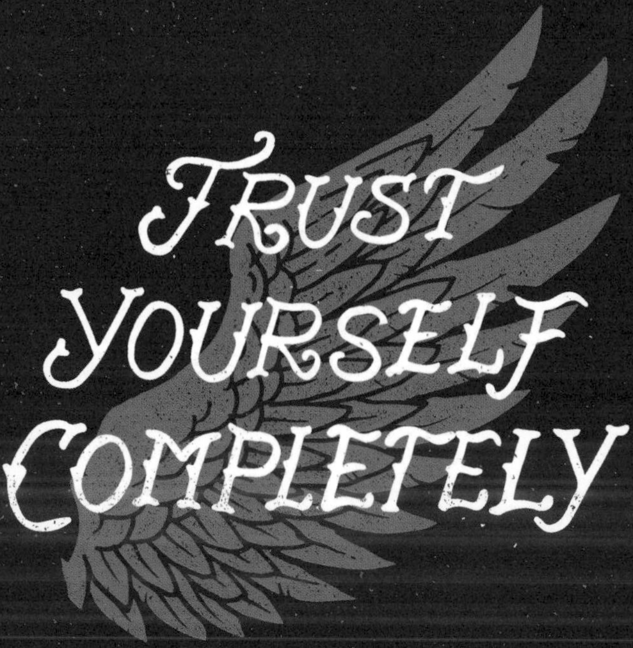
TRUST
YOURSELF
COMPLETELY

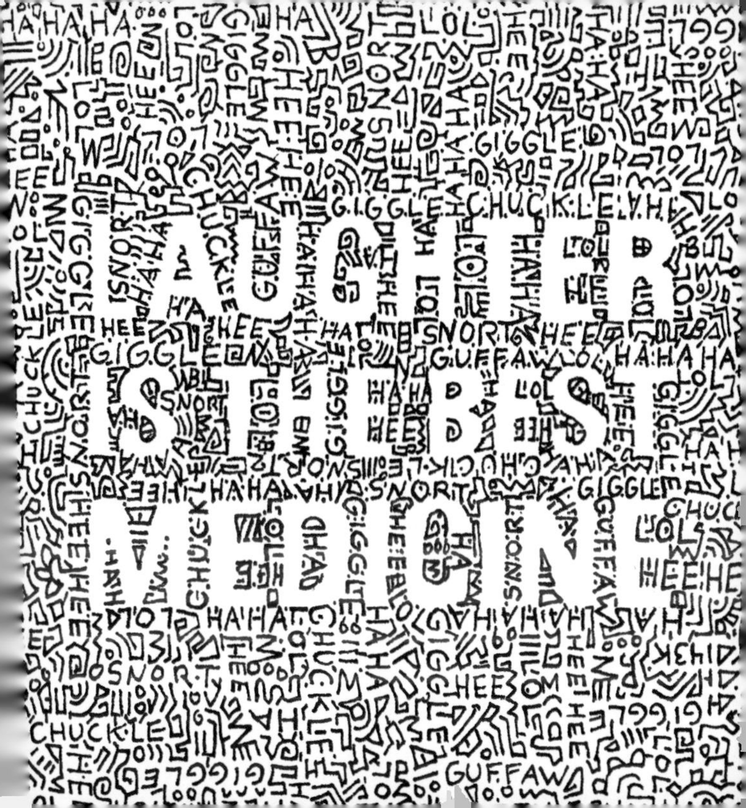
LAUGHTER
IS THE BEST
MEDICINE

Let Your soul Shine

START YOUR DAY WITH A DANCE PARTY

HOW **WONDERFUL** IT IS THAT NOBODY NEED WAIT A SINGLE MOMENT BEFORE STARTING TO IMPROVE THE WORLD

—ANNE FRANK

Even God has a sense of humor.
Just look at the platypus.

-Kevin Smith

HAPPINESS CAN BE FOUND even in the DARKEST of TIMES if one ONLY REMEMBERS to turn on THE LIGHT

—Albus Dumbledore

Few things soothe the soul like a warm cup of tea

You put the Shine in Sunshine

TO *live on purpose,*
follow your heart
AND *live your*
dreams

—MARCIA
WIEDER

IT'S
COMFORT
FOOD
O'CLOCK

getting **LOST** *may be the way* TO **FIND** YOURSELF

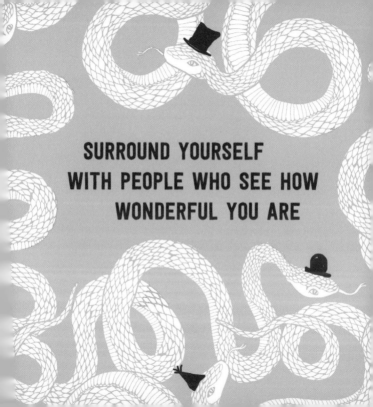

SURROUND YOURSELF
WITH PEOPLE WHO SEE HOW
WONDERFUL YOU ARE

TODAY YOU ARE YOU,

THAT IS TRUER THAN TRUE.

THERE IS NO ONE ALIVE

WHO IS YOUER THAN YOU.

~DR. SEUSS, *HAPPY BIRTHDAY TO YOU!*

STAY *gold*

—THE OUTSIDERS

BELIEVE IN YOURSELF

EAT SOME CHOCOLATE CAKE TODAY!

PREPARE ACCORDINGLY.

WHO IS THE *happier* MAN?
HE WHO **BRAVED** THE
Storm OF *Life*
AND **LIVED**—OR HE **WHO**
STAYED SECURELY ON
Shore AND MERELY
EXISTED?

~~~~~~~~

Hunter S. Thompson

KID, YOU'LL MOVE

MOUNTAINS!

today is your day!

YOUR MOUNTAIN

IS WAITING.

so get on your way!

— Dr. Seuss

Joy is a choice~
a great
one!

I AM
SO HAPPY
I TRIED
SOMETHING
NEW!

—YOU, TOMORROW

GREAT THINGS ARE JUST THE CORNER

ONE SMALL ACT
OF KINDNESS CAN
CHANGE THE WORLD

MAKE AN EFFORT
to feel
PROUD
of yourself
TODAY

Throw kindness around like

confetti

add a little
EXTRA
to your
ORDINARY

Let the world see you SHINE

LET'S FIND A PLACE TO GET LOST

Wave your SMILE as your own personal flag

you make me happy when skies are gray

BREAK
OUT
OF YOUR
COMFORT
ZONE

It's a
good day
to have a
good day

YOU ARE MORE THAN *Good* *Enough*

A little kindness can go a long way

YOUR THINKING

CHANGE

YOUR LIFE

Be truthful, gentle, and

FEARLESS.

—Mahatma Gandhi

Love is that condition in which the **happiness** of another person is essential to your own

- ROBERT HEINLEIN -

LIFE

was meant to be

LIVED, & CURIOSITY

MUST BE KEPT ALIVE.

ONE MUST NEVER,

for whatever reason,

TURN HIS BACK

on LIFE.

·ELEANOR ROOSEVELT·

No man is lonely while eating

SPAGHETTI

—Christopher Morley

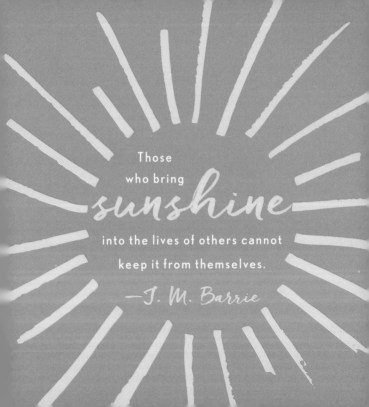

Those
who bring
sunshine
into the lives of others cannot
keep it from themselves.
—J. M. Barrie

BIG
THINGS
often
COME FROM
SMALL
BEGINNINGS

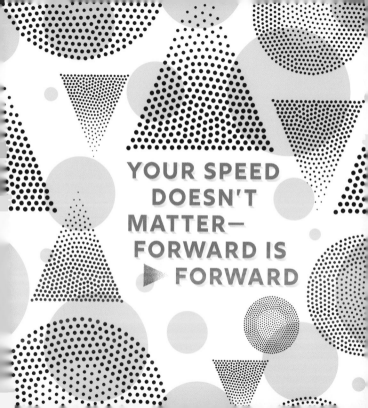

SOMETIMES YOU NEED TO **SINK** ALL THE WAY TO THE BOTTOM OF THE POOL TO **SHOOT OUT** OF THE WATER

DOUBT

KILLS

MORE

dreams

THAN

FAILURE

EVER

WILL

—suzy kassem

Life is Good

LIFE IS EITHER

A DARING ADVENTURE OR NOTHING

—HELEN KELLER

I URGE YOU TO PLEASE NOTICE WHEN

You are happy

+ EXCLAIM _____

_____ or MURMUR _____

_____ or THINK

· AT SOME POINT, "IF THIS ISN'T NICE, ·

I don't know what is."

KURT VONNEGUT

LIFE MIGHT NOT ALWAYS BE *perfect*, BUT IF *you look* HARD ENOUGH, YOU WILL SEE IT IS ALWAYS *magical*

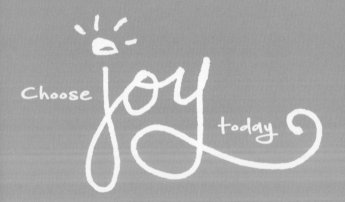
Choose joy today

BE SOMEONE'S ★

HERO

★ ★ ★

There is no
Beauty
without some
Strangeness

~ Edgar Allan Poe

Be happy
for this moment.
This moment
is your life.

C'est La Vie

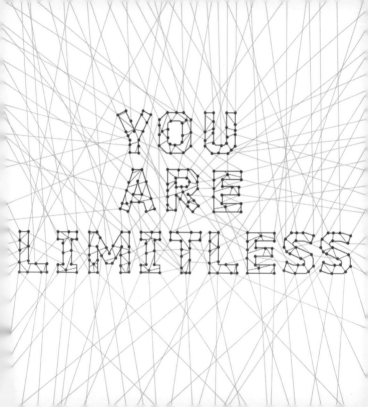

know your worth

DON'T
STOP
UNTIL
YOU'RE
PROUD

there can't be *flowers* without rain

Life moves pretty fast. If you don't STOP and **look** around once in awhile, you could *miss* it.

—ferris Bueller

NOTHING TURNS A
BAD MOOD
INTO A *good one*
FASTER THAN
CHOCOLATE

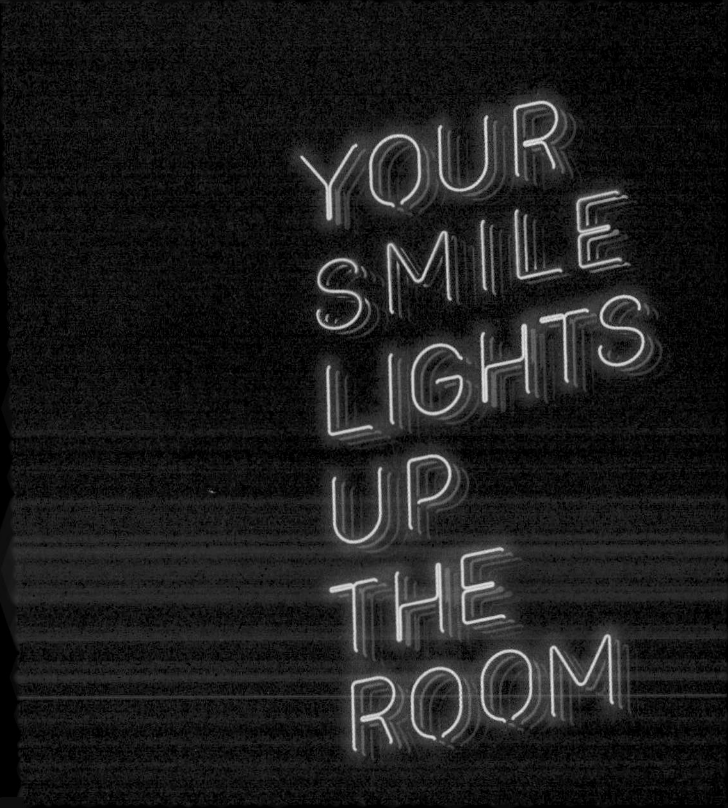
YOUR
SMILE
LIGHTS
UP
THE
ROOM

THE
SWEETEST *joy,*
THE WILDEST WOE IS
LOVE.

—PEARL
BAILEY

I'd far rather be happy than right any day.

Douglas Adams

If you spend too much time
searching for the perfect life,
you might miss the fact
that you already have one

THAT *smile* LOOKS GREAT ON YOU

"BEAUTY IS IN THE EYE OF THE BEHOLDER AND IT MAY BE NECESSARY FROM TIME TO TIME TO GIVE A STUPID OR MISINFORMED BEHOLDER A BLACK EYE."

—MISS PIGGY

Every day is the **PERFECT DAY** to **BINGE WATCH** a season **OF YOUR FAVORITE show**

THROW YOUR PARTY PANTS

ON!

SHARE THE LOVE

TAKE TIME TO
MAKE YOUR
SOUL
HAPPY

strive to be
present
in every aspect
of your life

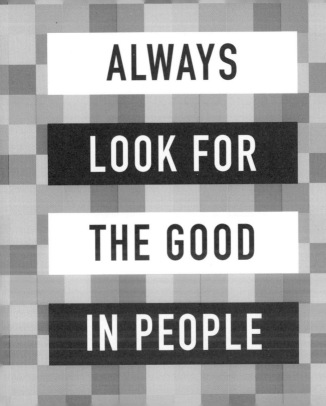

collect new experiences

friendship
isn't a
big thing

it's a
million little
things

-anonymous

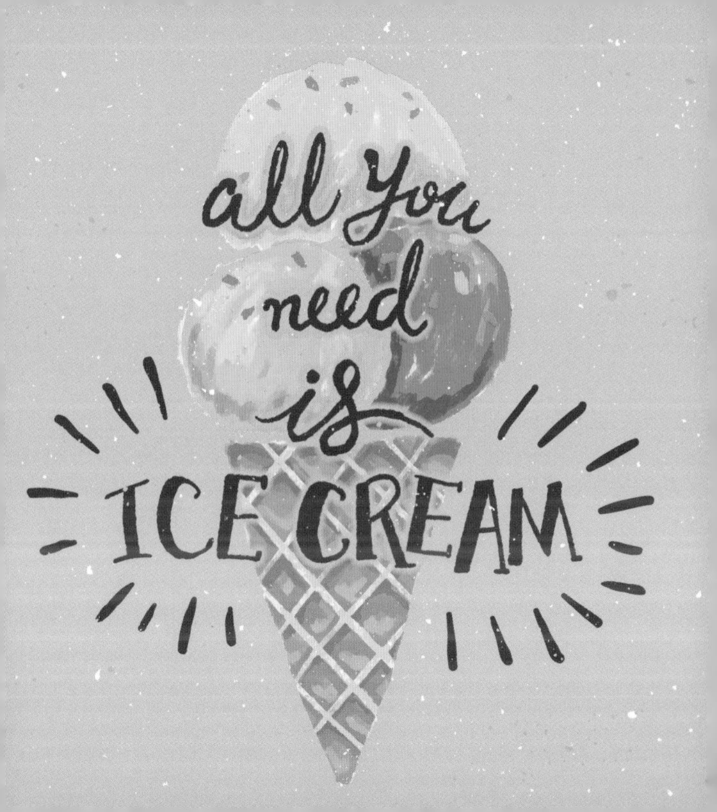
all you
need
is
ICE CREAM

DARE TO LIVE
THE LIFE YOU HAVE
DREAMED FOR YOURSELF.
GO FORWARD AND MAKE
YOUR DREAMS COME TRUE.

—RALPH WALDO EMERSON

be

BOLD

A good laugh
and a long sleep
are the two best
CURES *FOR* ANYTHING

IRISH PROVERB

YOU'RE A

Real

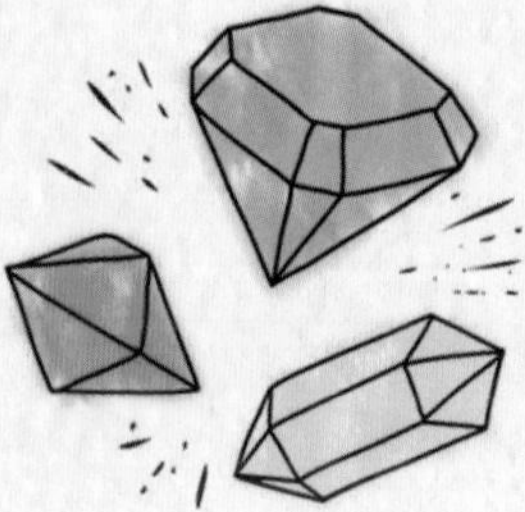

GEM

I THINK IF YOU CAN DANCE AND BE FREE
AND NOT EMBARRASSED, YOU CAN RULE THE WORLD

—AMY POEHLER

you
are
loved

TREAT YOURSELF to an ice cream sundae: something about SPRINKLES, Hot Fudge, & whipped cream CAN MAKE ANYONE smile.

DANCE BREAK!

MAKE SILLY FACES.
THEY WON'T STAY
LIKE THAT FOREVER,
NO MATTER WHAT YOUR
MOTHER TOLD YOU.

Hello, SUNSHINE!

happiness is a habit

IF YOU STUMBLE,
MAKE IT PART
OF THE DANCE

TAKE A MOMENT AND
THINK ABOUT ALL YOU HAVE.
JOY STARTS WITH A GRATEFUL

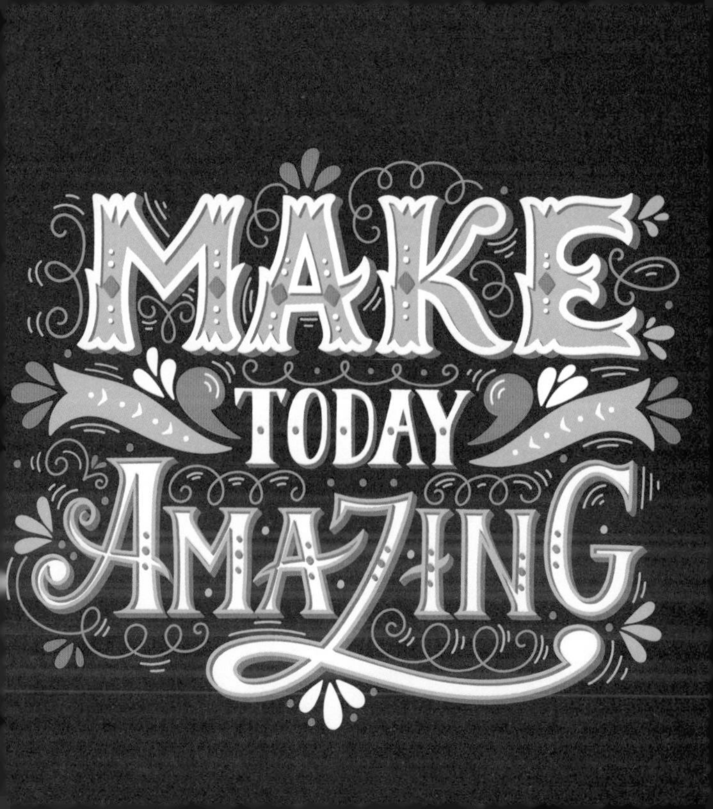
MAKE
TODAY
AMAZING

ONCE YOU CHOOSE

hope,

ANYTHING

IS

Possible

—CHRISTOPHER REEVE

BE SILLY.
BE HONEST.
BE KIND.

—RALPH WALDO EMERSON

decisions

DETERMINE

destiny

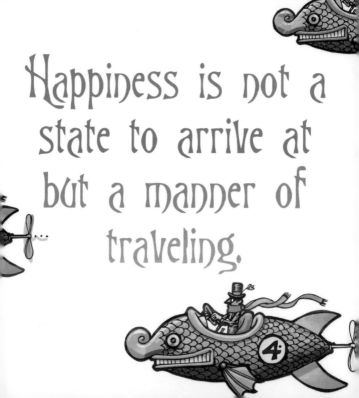

Happiness is not a state to arrive at but a manner of traveling.

EVERY DAY IS
AN OPPORTUNITY TO
LEARN SOMETHING NEW

sMILES

ARE ALWAYS TRENDING

Happiness IS NOT A destination. IT IS A method of life

— BURTON HILLS

IN A WORLD WHERE YOU CAN BE ANYTHING

be kind.

YOU ARE THE UNDISPUTED WORLD CHAMPION OF BEING YOU

IF YOU'RE LOOKING TO THE FUTURE,

PUT ON SOME SHADES— YOUR FUTURE IS GOING TO BE

Bright

Be WHO YOU were
Born
TO
Be

A LITTLE MAGIC

CAN TAKE YOU A LONG WAY

-ROALD DAHL

Cherish

THE

SIMPLE THINGS

Beautiful Minds Inspire others

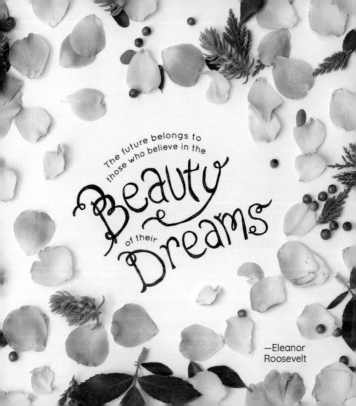

The future belongs to those who believe in the *Beauty* of their *Dreams*

—Eleanor Roosevelt

if more of us VALUED FOOD and CHEER & Song ABOVE HOARDED GOLD, *it would be* A MERRIER WORLD.

~ J. R. R. Tolkien ~

IF there is NO STRUGGLE, THERE is NO PROGRESS

Frederick Douglass

Don't let the unknown intimidate you

YOU have to go a little **CRAZY** every once in a while to stay **SANE**

You do you, you're a natural at it.

take some time to
catch up with an old friend

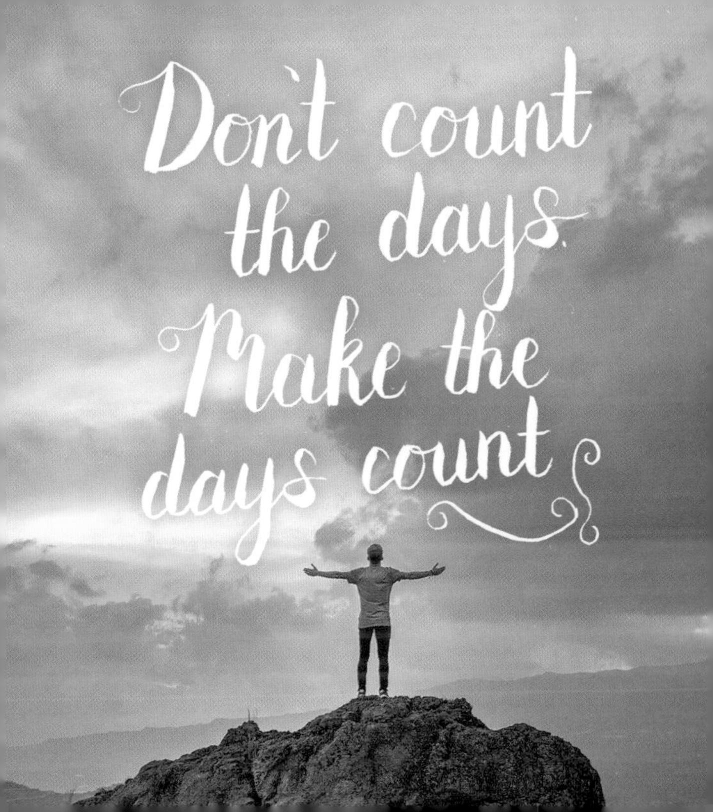
Don't count the days.
Make the days count

Creativity IS intelligence HAVING fun

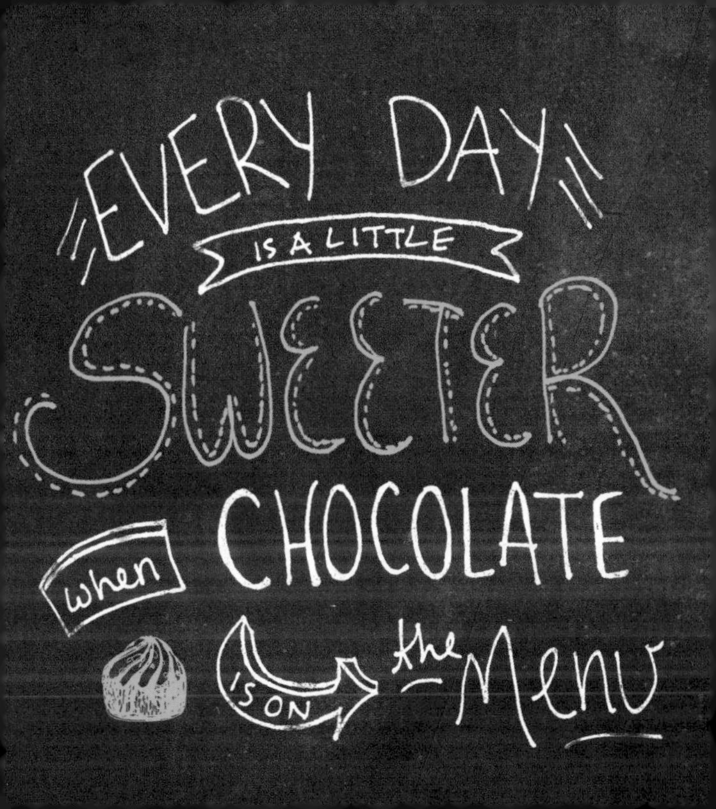

EVERY DAY
IS A LITTLE
SWEETER
when
CHOCOLATE
IS ON
the
Menu

LIFE IS TOO
SHORT
TO NOT
EXPRESS
YOURSELF

MAKE SOMEONE ELSE HAPPY,
AND YOUR OWN HAPPINESS
WILL WORK ITSELF OUT

LIFE IS TOO SHORT TO BE bored

you are

SERIOUSLY
GREAT

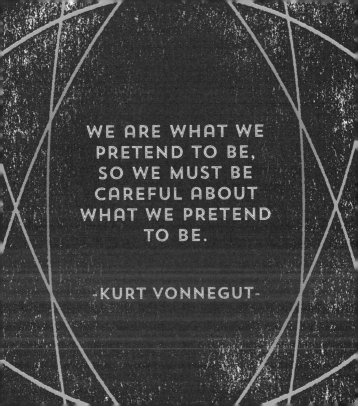

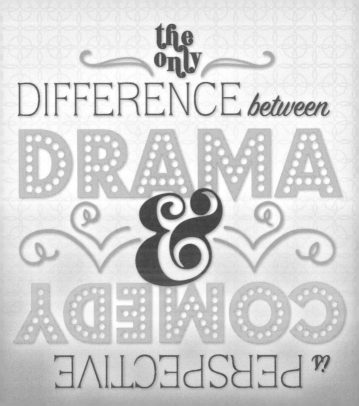

the only DIFFERENCE *between* DRAMA & COMEDY *is* a PERSPECTIVE

Be your own
YOU!

HAPPINESS
ISN'T SOMETHING
YOU PURSUE.
IT'S SOMETHING
YOU DO!

be a *flamingo* in a flock of pigeons

be a
GOOFBALL
every once in a while

Do more of what makes you happy

live.
LAUGH.
LOVE.
(REPEAT.)

LIFE ISN'T ABOUT FINDING YOURSELF.
LIFE IS ABOUT CREATING YOURSELF.

—GEORGE BERNARD SHAW—

take time to SMELL the Roses

you are

BRAVER than you BELIEVE,
STRONGER than you SEEM,
and SMARTER

than you

THINK.

—A. A. Milne,
Winnie-the-Pooh

PEOPLE WHO *love* TO EAT ARE THE BEST PEOPLE

-JULIA CHILD

time you enjoy wasting is not wasted time

MARTHE TROLY-CURTIN

EVERYTHING IS BETTER IF IT HAPPENS IN A

BLANKET FORT

GRIN

and

SHARE IT

LET SOMEONE KNOW
YOU LOVE THEM,
EVEN IF THAT
SOMEONE
IS YOURSELF

SOMETIMES
ALL IT TAKES
TO TURN A
BAD DAY INTO
A GREAT ONE
IS A LITTLE
POSITIVITY

THE WORLD IS A BETTER PLACE BECAUSE YOU'RE IN IT

RECHARGE
YOUR
MIND

A DAY WITHOUT LAUGHTER IS A DAY WASTED

The Artists!

John Aardema (33, 85, 123, 165, 181, 197, 237, 267, 277, 289, 377); Bridget M. Alexander (141); Elizabeth Boyer (341); Susan Busch (223, 387); Catherine Casalino Design (11); Jennifer K. Beal Davis (27, 121, 273); Matt Davis (29, 139); Maggie Edkins (23, 47); Cassie Gutman (39, 97, 175, 219, 225, 241, 263, 331, 367); Travis Hasenour (61, 117, 147, 205, 211, 321, 343, 363); Nicole Hower (305); Krista Joy Johnson (53, 345); Kelly Lawler (99, 113, 129, 179, 255); Michelle McAvoy (35, 229, 249, 271, 365); Danielle McNaughton (69, 103, 119, 153, 257, 301, 311); Lin Miceli (17, 185, 215); Benjamin Nelson (31); Kay Birkner (55, 157, 189, 213, 283, 325); Heather Morris (9, 73, 111, 167, 177, 183, 203, 217, 227, 245, 253, 275, 285, 315, 323, 355, 373, 383, 391); Bethany Orlowski (7); Ben Ouart (1, 95, 163, 293); Jenna Quatraro (45, 297, 339); Jillian Rahn (49, 77, 87, 125, 131, 155, 193, 207, 313, 349); Kerri Resnick (137); Kandi Rich (15, 327, 351); Tina Silva (5, 51, 101, 169); Becca Sage (243); Eliza Smith (59, 71, 107, 353); Allison Sundstrom (3, 21, 145, 209, 369, 375); Amanda Skolek (65, 75, 359); Brittany Vibbert (37, 43, 57, 63, 67, 81, 83, 89, 91, 93, 105, 115, 127, 133, 135, 143, 149, 151, 159, 173, 187, 191, 195, 199, 201, 231, 239, 251, 259, 261, 265, 279, 281, 295, 299, 309, 317, 319, 329, 333, 335, 337, 347, 357, 361, 379, 381, 385, 389, 393); Christine Webster (19, 79, 233)